Lo que mi abuela me dijo

※≫ ⎯ ≪※

What My Grandmother Told Me

Lo que mi abuela me dijo

What My Grandmother Told Me

PRACTICAL WISDOM FROM SPANISH PROVERBS AND SAYINGS

Maria Paz Eleizegui Weir

Illustrations by MAHALA URRA

University of New Mexico • Press Albuquerque

Text © 2015 by Maria Paz Eleizegui Weir and Ilaw ng Tahanan Publishing, Inc.
Illustrations © 2015 by Mahala Urra and Ilaw ng Tahanan Publishing, Inc.
University of New Mexico Press edition published 2016 by arrangement with Tahanan
Books, a division of Ilaw ng Tahanan Publishing, Inc.
Printed in South Korea
20 19 18 17 16   1 2 3 4 5

Library of Congress Cataloging-in-Publication Data
Weir, Maria Paz Eleizegui.
  Lo que mi abuela me dijo/what my grandmother told me : practical wisdom from Spanish
proverbs and sayings / Maria Paz Eleizegui Weir ; illustrations by Mahala Urra.
     pages cm
  ISBN 978-0-8263-5634-5 (pbk. : alk. paper) — ISBN 978-0-8263-5635-2 (electronic)
  1. Proverbs, Spanish. I. Urra, Mahala. II. Title. III. Title: What my grandmother told me.
  PN6491.W45 2016
  398.9'61—dc23

                              2015020161

Cover illustration: Mahala Urra

Book design and vignettes by Auri Asuncion Yambao
Color work by Grace Asuncion and Auri Asuncion Yambao

❧ CONTENTS ❧

INTRODUCTION

ix

La voz de mi abuela / The Voice of My Grandmother

x

I *Juventud* / Childhood

1

II *Amistad* / Friendship

33

III *Comportamiento* / Manners

67

IV *Lucha y trabajo* / Work and Strife

89

V *Sabiduría* / Wisdom

127

VI *Amor y destino* / Love and Destiny

157

Las lagrimas de mi abuela / The Tears of My Grandmother

188

ACKNOWLEDGMENTS

194

A mi abuelita—
aunque ya se fue, siempre está conmigo

To my grandmother—
who has departed, yet is always with me

⚜ INTRODUCTION ⚜

I grew up listening to my grandmother's voice as often as my favorite melodies playing on the radio. Although the words were usually her own, what I remember best are the Spanish proverbs that she often quoted, adding flavor to her speech, like salt and pepper in everyday meals. She sincerely believed that *dichos*, with their unique blend of sound and sense, delivered important messages of useful and lasting value. Over time, she hoped, they would inspire me to lead a better life. Which is just what they did, and why I remember them to this day.

If any *dichos* in this book sound familiar to you, perhaps you heard them from a friend, or a relative, long ago. Maybe you even know a version spoken in your own country. The language may be different, but their intent and meaning are the same. Like our favorite songs, their melodies linger on, reminding us that wisdom transcends time and has no borders.

Maria Paz Eleizegui Weir

La voz de mi abuela

The Voice of My Grandmother

When you are almost four years old and can slip into your pajama bottoms all by yourself or tie your shoelaces without any help, life is full of possibilities. Some appear as unexpectedly as a heavy downpour on a hot afternoon in Manila. On such a day, I was taken to visit my grandparents who lived in a big house nearby, on a street called Calle Wright. "For a few days," I was told, but I remained there until I was twelve. Like a green mango plucked from the tree and made to ripen elsewhere.

Because we were a Spanish-speaking family, they called me *Chiquita* (small) while I was a tiny baby. I chopped the last syllable from my nickname as soon as I could—and became *Chiquita* forever. The name does not appear on my passport or on my driver's license. But it's the one I like best.

You have to go back to your childhood to find out who you are. Mine (the part worth remembering) began the day I arrived on Calle Wright. It was a steamy May afternoon. I stood on my grandparents' veranda, wiping my tears with a giant towel draped over my shoulders to keep me dry, when I heard my grandmother's voice. "Listen to your *abuelita*," she was saying, *"No hay mal que por bien no venga."* It was the first of many Spanish *dichos*, colorful sayings she would quote long before I understood what they meant. Misfortunes do happen, at times by necessity, because something good will turn up in the end.

At that moment, it was like seeing my grandmother for the first time; her soft eyes framed by round rimless glasses, her back straight as a pole even while she looked down at me. She wore a loose-flowing dress that went down to her knees and had a hair comb edged in gold that glistened when she turned her head. Her voice was calm and reassuring. I can hear it in my mind today, as clearly as a digital recording. With nothing more to say, my parents left casually, as if they would return the next day. The black wrought-iron gate of 904 Wright Street closed with the sound of metal scraping against the cement sidewalk, like a mournful ache. I tugged at my grandmother's skirt while she rearranged the pots of maidenhair fern decorating the veranda.

The world of Calle Wright with its happy mixture of generations was the right place to be. I had a grandfather who took me on Sunday-afternoon drives in his gleaming black Packard sedan, and whose generous impulses drove him to buy me five pairs of shoes when only one was needed. *"Aguarda pan para Mayo,"* said my grandmother, and sent four of them back. My middle-aged aunt always kept a close eye on me while drifting about the house doing household duties. Her favorite fragrance, *Je Reviens,* surrounded her like a mist, alerting everyone that she was coming. A younger aunt, widely recognized as a former Miss Philippines, was fond of clinging silk dresses. I liked watching her descend, with high-heeled sandals clicking, down the winding staircase. If no one was looking, I tried swaying my hips the way she did before taking a gentleman's arm as they walked toward the front door.

The move to Calle Wright was never explained to me. Perhaps, as the saying goes, *"Lo que se ve no se pregunta."* What is obvious hardly needs to be explained. Besides, my parents came often, so their absence was scarcely felt. Filipinos take great pride in connectedness to family, with its large web of distant relatives. Most of my aunts, uncles, and cousins were in the same neighborhood, living in adjoining duplexes or in similar houses separated by a courtyard, like leaves that fell from the same tree and landed next to each other.

What my *abuelita* told me on that afternoon of sun and rain found a permanent home in my memory. The *dichos* she often repeated cast their own unique spell by revealing essential truths that I needed to hear. Best of all, they were told by a grandmother who spoke with the one true voice—the voice of the heart.

With a strong sense of relief, I ran out to play. *Abuelita's* voice could be heard echoing in the distance. *"Cuidado, cuidado."* Be careful, she was saying almost in rhythm with my steps. It was a joyful day, full of promise. I would soon be four years old. I knew how to use a jumping rope. And I had learned to count up to three.

Juventud

I

Childhood

Cada casa es un misterio.

Every house holds a mystery.

Al que madruga,
Dios le ayuda.

God rewards early risers.

Lo que se aprende en la
cuna siempre dura.

What is learned in the cradle
lasts through life.

Genio y figura,
hasta la sepultura.

Looks and personality
accompany you to the grave.

Lo que en los libros no está,
la vida te enseñará.

What is not in your textbooks,
you will learn from life.

Echando a perder
se aprende.

You can learn a lesson
with every loss.

El saber no ocupa lugar.

There is always room for learning.

La educación es la única cosa
que nadie te podrá quitar.

Education is the only thing
no one can take away from you.

El que no llora no mama.

A child who doesn't cry, doesn't get fed.

El árbol que crece torcido
nunca su rama se endereza.

You cannot straighten
the trunk of a crooked tree.

Si a tu hijo no le das castigo,
serás su peor enemigo.

An unpunished child
can become your worst enemy.

De tal palo, tal astilla.

It's a chip off the old block.

Primero el deber
y luego el placer.

Duty first, pleasure later.

Para tonto no se estudia.

Being dumb
does not require lessons.

Quien no oye consejo,
no llega a viejo.

You don't gain wisdom
and reach old age without
listening to advice.

Más vale prevenir que lamentar.

Better to prevent than to lament.

Aguarda pan para mayo.

Do not eat all your bread
in one day.

Quien bien te quiere
te hará llorar.

Who loves you best
also makes you cry.

Amistad

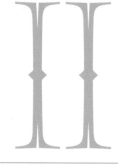

II

Friendship

A buen amigo,
buen abrigo.

A good friend is as comforting
as a warm coat.

En la necesidad
se conoce la amistad.

———————— ⁓ ————————

True friends are with you
when you need them.

Hoy por ti, mañana por mí.

Today for you—tomorrow for me.
(One good turn deserves another.)

El favor recibido debe ser correspondido.

Favors received should be repaid.

Cuentas claras
conservan amistades.

———— ⚬ ————

Making things clear
preserves friendships.

Haz el bien, y no mires a quién.

Do good without concern
for whom you do it.

Si quieres el perro, acepta las pulgas.

If you like the dog, accept the fleas.

———— ❧ ————

Sarna que te gusta no pica.

An itch that pleases seldom bothers you.

El que presta a un amigo,
pierde el dinero y pierde el amigo.

Loan money to a friend,
and you may lose your money,
as well as your friend.

No digas todo lo que sepas,
ni des todo lo que tengas.

Do not say everything you know,
nor give everything you have.

En boca cerrada
no entran moscas.

Flies do not enter a closed mouth.

La gracia de la fea,
la bonita lo desea.

Beautiful women desire
the grace and good nature
of someone who is plain.

No hagas cosas malas
que a la vista parecen buenas.

Do not do wrong things
that appear to be good.

Agua que no has de beber,
déjala correr.

If it is water you don't want
to drink, let it run.

*La amistad hace lo que la
sangre no hace.*

Friendship binds us more
than blood ties.

*Parientes tiene uno,
pero amigos se pueden escoger.*

You can choose your friends
but not your relatives.

Dime con quién andas
y te diré quién eres.

———— ⟋⟍ ————

Tell me about your friends
and I'll tell you who you are.
(You are known by
the company you keep.)

*Más vale estar sola que
mal acompañada.*

Better to be alone
than in poor company.

Vida sin amigos,
muerte sin testigos.

Life without friends
is death by solitude.

Comportamiento

III

Manners

Calladita te ves más bonita.

A quiet little girl
appears prettier and sweeter.
(Silence is golden.)

Consejo no pedido,
consejo mal oído.

Advice that is not asked
should not be given.

De la mano a la boca,
se pierde la sopa.

———— ⚬ ————

Soup can spill before
it reaches your mouth.
(Accidents can happen.)

Lo que es moda no incomoda.

What is trendy always has a following.

Sobre gustos no hay nada escrito.

Nothing is sacred in matters of taste.

Hay gustos que
merecen palos.

Some people have tastes
that deserve a good spanking!

Una cosa es la instrucción
y otra es la educación.

It's one thing to be instructed
and another to be educated.

Mono vestido de seda,
mono se queda.

A monkey dressed in silk
is still a monkey.

Los trapos sucios se lavan en casa.

Dirty linen is washed at home.

A mal tiempo buena cara.

In bad times, put up a good face.

Se dice el pecado pero no el pecador.

Reveal the sin but not the sinner.

Pagan justos por pecadores.

Sometimes the just have to pay
for the sinners.

*Lo cortés no quita nada
a lo valiente.*

Courtesy does not deprive you of valor.

Lucha y trabajo

IV

Work and Strife

Querer es poder.

If you want to, you can do it.

Si vale la pena hacerlo,
vale la pena hacerlo bien.

If it's worth doing,
it's worth doing well.

*Si quieres dinero y
fama, que no te agarre
el sol de la mañana.*

If you want money and fame,
don't let the sun catch you in bed.

No hay que empezar la
casa por el tejado.

Do not build your roof
before the rest of the house.

Más puede maña que fuerza.

Brain is better than brawn.

Escoba nueva barre bien.

A new broom sweeps better.

Excava el pozo
antes de que tengas sed.

Dig the well
before you are thirsty.

*Del dicho al hecho
hay mucho trecho.*

The distance between
saying and doing—is immense.

El trabajo compartido
es más llevadero.

Work that is shared
is easier to complete.

*No hay peor lucha de la que
no se hace.*

The worst struggle is the one
you did not begin.

Por el dinero baila el perro.

For money, even the dog will dance.

Murió el perro, y se acabó la rabia.

The rabies are ended when the dog is dead.

Una llave de oro abre cualquier puerta.

A gold key will open any door.

No es más rico el que tiene,
sino el que menos necesita.

Those who need less are richer
than those who always need more.

Aunque la jaula es de oro,
no deja de ser prisión.

Even if the cage is gold, it can still be a prison.

Quiere pescar sin mojarse las nalgas.

Some like to fish without getting wet.

Con su pan se lo coma.

Let him eat his own bread.

Cada uno sabe donde
le aprieta el zapato.

Only the owner knows
where the shoe pinches.

Camarón que se duerme
acaba en la paella.

———— ❧ ————

A sleeping shrimp ends up
in a dish of paella.

Despacio se va lejos.

You cover more distance
if you don't speed.

No hay curva mala
pasándola despacio.

No curve is too sharp
if taken slowly.

A Dios rogando
y con el mazo dando.

———— ❦ ————

Praise God
but keep on hammering.

Sabiduría

Wisdom

Antes de hacer nada,
consúltalo con la almohada.

Before doing anything,
consult your pillow.

Cobra buena fama
y échate a dormir.

Establish a good reputation,
then go to sleep.

La mayor felicidad
es la conformidad.

Acceptance is a major key
to happiness.

No escupas al cielo
porque a la cara te cae.

Don't spit at the sky
or it may land on your face.

De médico, poeta, y loco,
todos tenemos un poco.

There is a bit of the doctor,
the poet, and the madman
in all of us.

*Más sabe el diablo
por viejo que por diablo.*

The devil knows more because he is old
than because he is the devil.

Lo que se ve no se pregunta.

What is obvious needs no explanation.

*Del árbol caído
todos hacen leña.*

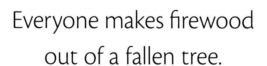

Everyone makes firewood
out of a fallen tree.

No hay más ciego del
que no quiere ver.

No one is more blind
than someone who refuses to see.

Es el mismo perro
con diferente collar.

It's the same dog
with a different collar.

Cada loco tiene su tema.

Every fool has a different theme.

───────── ❦ ─────────

*No se puede tapar
el sol con un dedo.*

You cannot shield the sun
with one finger.

A falta de pan buenas son tortas.

When you have no bread,
cake will do.

No todo lo que brilla es oro.

Not everything that shines is gold.

Nunca digas de este vaso no beberé.

Never say from this glass I will not drink.

No te ahogues en un vaso de agua.

Don't let yourself drown in a glass of water.

Dios aprieta pero no ahoga.

God squeezes but does not choke.

Amor y destino

VI

Love and Destiny

*Los pies siguen
donde va el corazón.*

Where the heart goes,
the feet will follow.

Algunos nacen con estrella
y otros nacen estrellados.

Some are born under a lucky star;
others are born shattered.

*El hombre propone
y Dios dispone.*

Man proposes
and God disposes.

No hay mal que por bien
no venga.

No setback happens
without a hidden benefit.

Ojos que no ven,
corazón que no siente.

What the eyes do not see,
the heart does not feel.

Caras vemos,
corazones no sabemos.

Faces we can see;
hearts we cannot fathom.

Cada oveja con su pareja.

Every sheep has its partner;
they keep to their own kind.

Donde hubo llamas,
cenizas quedan.

If there were flames,
there could still be embers.

Un clavo saca otro clavo.

One nail can pull out another nail.
(A lost love can be replaced
with another romance.)

Donde hay amor,
hay dolor.

———— ❧ ————

Where there is love,
there is pain.

Cuando la pobreza entra
por la puerta, el amor
sale por la ventana.

When poverty enters the door,
love escapes through the window.

Antes de que te cases,
mira lo que haces.

———— ✦ ————

Before you marry,
be sure you know what you're doing.

Casamiento y mortaja
del cielo baja.

Marriage and death
come from heaven.

No dejes camino por vereda.

Do not abandon the road to your
destination by taking another path.

La distancia y el tiempo
causa olvido.

Time and distance bring forgetfulness.

*Las hojas en el árbol
no duran toda la vida.*

The leaves on the tree
do not last forever.

Amor con amor se paga.

———— ⧯ ————

Love is repaid with love.

Las lagrimas de mi abuela

The Tears of My Grandmother

Pregúntale a las estrellas si por las noches me ven llorar
Ask the stars if at night they see me cry
(Opening line of my grandmother's favorite song)

When you are almost thirteen, growing up seems to take forever. Childhood was like baby clothes that I outgrew and were replaced almost every year. I no longer danced with my feet perched on my grandfather's shoes as he guided me around the shiny living-room floor. In school I spoke English and studied from textbooks that read "Printed in USA" My favorite reading place was the family bathroom, which was a good place to hide until my grandmother's hurried "*¡Apúrate!*" followed by several knocks on the carved mahogany door began to sound like thunder. At times I wondered about living in a land of apple trees instead of coconut groves. I even wished that the Pasig River would freeze so I could learn to skate on a smooth sheet of ice.

What continued as reliably as the ticking of the clock on my bedside table was the echo of my grandmother's teachings. "*El saber no ocupa lugar,*" she always said. Learning is never out of place. The thought of my being away from her world did not disturb her whenever I spoke of going to school in another country. I was only twelve years old, she often reminded me, "*Del dicho al hecho, hay mucho trecho.*" It's a long way between what you say and what you do. "Remember," she added, "the unexpected happens."

A week after that curious remark, my parents arrived for the usual Sunday dinner in Calle Wright with surprising news. The family was seated at the round outdoor table under the *kalachuchi* tree, its blossoms brilliant under the sun. Beside us a giant electric fan stirred the air, discouraging flies from hovering over trays of Spanish stew. "*Ya es tiempo.*" It's time, my father said, to be at home. He repeated "at home" several times, without realizing that I was already where I belonged.

I did not see tears behind my grandmother's lenses, but I knew they were there. She was serene and poised, like the image on her wedding portrait with my grandfather standing next to her looking stately in black tie and tails. Nothing else was said. That night I was fearful and slept next to my *abuelita*. As if lying there, beside her, would stretch the hours and prolong my stay. Familiar lines from her favorite song kept repeating inside my head like a damaged record with a needle stuck in one of its grooves. *"No olvides nunca que yo te quiero."* Never forget that I care for you. It was somebody's love song, with words that sounded as if they were written for me. Years later I asked her why she made no effort to keep me. *"Abuelita,"* I cried out, "You knew how much I wanted to stay!" She replied, quoting one of her *dichos. "Lo cortés no quita a lo valiente."* Being courteous does not mean you lack courage. "If you have to make a decision, it is best to do what is noble."

When news that I was awarded a scholarship in the United States reached my grandmother, she took me aside. "People will say you should not leave your *abuelita*. I am old and may never see you again. But, if that is what you truly want," she said, pointing her finger emphatically, "then I tell you to go."

I hid my excitement, weeping with abandon like a heroine in a Mexican telenovela, unaware of the price my grandmother paid to set me free. Her remarks that I once treated casually, today bring an awareness of common sense and real sorrow. *"En la vida,"* she told me, *"las cosas baratas,* like cars and jewelry, you buy with money. Expensive things, *como el amor y la obligación, se pagan con las emociones y el sacrificio.* In life, what is costly, like love and devotion, is paid with your emotions and with sacrifice."

The day before my departure, she tucked a carefully wrapped package in my overstuffed Samsonite suitcase, already swelling like an overfed pig. Inside were items she was sure I would need to absorb the shock of an unfamiliar environment. Among them were six white linen handkerchiefs embroidered with her initial, similar to mine, since I was named after her. (The faint fragrance of sampaguita blossoms pressed between each layer was still there when I opened the package in Seattle.) Despite objections from my widely traveled aunts ("Everything is available in America!") she included a sewing kit with needles already threaded, an assortment of safety pins, and her favorite cure-all: a jar of Mentholatum ointment. I found little use for the sewing kit and the safety pins. But the soothing relief of Mentholatum, rubbed on my throat on a moist and chilly winter night, always brought the comforting memory of *Abuelita's* hand on my forehead, checking for signs of a fever.

It took years to understand why my life began, but did not end, in Calle Wright. I returned to Manila more than once after graduating, but I did not remain long. By the time my grandmother was gone, I was an American citizen with a secure future at the university. Remembering how much she meant to me, my dutiful Manila cousins forwarded her diamond engagement ring, a plant from her bedroom window, and her favorite rosary beads. The most memorable gift, the one with lasting value, was already with me. *Abuelita's* timeless *dichos* and the truths they revealed are mine forever. *"Nadie tiene la vida comprada."* Life is unpredictable. Unlike a book that can be bought and paid for, it has to be lived.

F I N

Maria Paz Eleizegui Weir

En tus apures y afanes
acude a los refranes.

When needs and difficulties arise
take refuge in the proverbs.

❊ ACKNOWLEDGMENTS ❊

Some very special people have my deep appreciation for their contribution toward bringing this book to life.

Warmest thanks to Reni Roxas, my co-creator and publisher, for turning a writing project into an unforgettable journey of the mind and heart.

Mahala Urra has my gratitude and admiration for visualizing my grandmother's words with sensitivity and insight. Thanks for adding humor and sparkle to the illustrations.

I'm extremely grateful for Auri Asuncion Yambao's artistic involvement. Her design wizardry has worked its magic on every page.

Maraming Salamat to Fran Ong, who walked many extra miles preparing the manuscript and whose tireless work ensured its progress.

Muchas Gracias to Manny Roxas for his list of well-remembered *dichos* that inspired us to begin our journey.

I'm deeply indebted to Roz Pape, for her mentorship and professional advice on publication matters. And most of all, for her continued interest and support.

Special thanks to my colleague and friend Michael Harvey for his editorial suggestions and encouragement.

I'm grateful to Larry Weir, my husband and staunchest ally, for his unswerving devotion to my cause, and for being "the wind beneath my wings."

Finally, a warm salute to Kathryn MacDonald, Iris Hodge, and all those who, through the years, have heard me repeat my grandmother's proverbs and said, "Put them in a book someday."